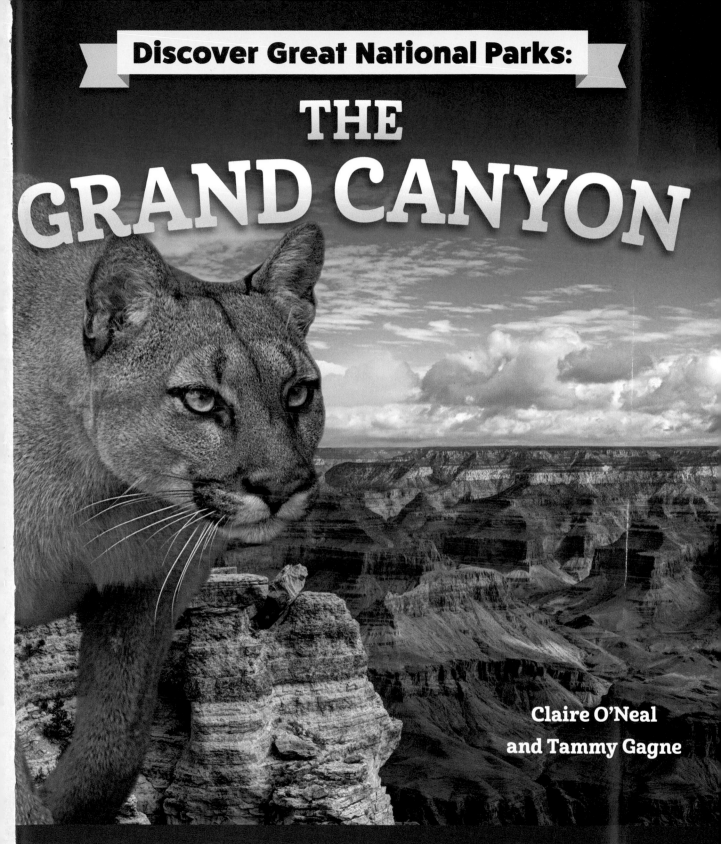

Discover Great National Parks:

THE
GRAND CANYON

Claire O'Neal
and Tammy Gagne

Kids' Guide to History, Wildlife, Trails, and Preservation

© 2024 by Curious Fox Books™, an imprint of Fox Chapel Publishing Company, Inc., 903 Square Street, Mount Joy, PA 17552.

Discover Great National Parks: Grand Canyon is a revision of *Grand Canyon*, published in 2017 by Purple Toad Publishing, Inc. Reproduction of its contents is strictly prohibited without written permission from the rights holder.

Paperback ISBN 979-8-89094-068-1
Hardcover ISBN 979-8-89094-069-8

The Cataloging-in-Publication Data in on file with the Library of Congress.

To learn more about the other great books from Fox Chapel Publishing, or to find a retailer near you, call toll-free 800-457-9112 or visit us at www.FoxChapelPublishing.com.

We are always looking for talented authors. To submit an idea, please send a brief inquiry to acquisitions@foxchapelpublishing.com.

Fox Chapel Publishing makes every effort to use environmentally friendly paper for printing.

Printed in China

WELCOME

Chapter One
MEET THE
CANYON

Maybe you drive there through the dry desert. Scrubby bushes, short pinyon pine trees, and some blooming prickly pears dot the flat sand. Washout valleys cut during heavy rains ripple between them. If you look in the distance, you may notice dark peaks. These volcanoes erupted ash and lava over the region less than a thousand years ago.[1] Otherwise, the ground is a plain.

Or maybe you come through a lush, pine-filled forest. Twisting, turning mountain roads continue to take you higher, making your ears pop. You roll down the window and smell fresh air and trees.

Suddenly, the road turns. The trees clear out. There's something odd about the land in front of you. It's as if there is no land. Your parents pull over, and you all get out to see it for yourself. In front of you lies a scar on the face of Earth itself. It looks as if a giant ax crashed down through the solid desert rock and split the world in two. You've never been here before, but you know, instantly, where you are. The Grand Canyon is unlike anywhere else on Earth.

The Grand Canyon's colorful striped cliffs can be enjoyed from almost any spot along its rim.

The Grand Canyon's two sides—the North and the South—are separated by the Colorado River. The gap between them is narrowest here at Marble Canyon.

The Grand Canyon stretches out before you on an unbelievable scale. No bridge can span this gorge. It's too far and too deep. At its narrowest, at Marble Canyon, only 600 feet separate its two sides. At its widest, the Grand Canyon yawns to eighteen miles across.[2] But most spectacular is the drop. On average, it's a mile straight down to the ribbon of river on the canyon floor. Some canyon walls have been shaped into shelves, mesas, plateaus, and temples. These features give the straight-sided canyon its wiggles and ripples. Other canyon walls are sheer cliffs, where one wrong step could mean a fall to your death. Whether sheer or shaped, Earth's insides are revealed in spectacular color. Rainbow layers of rock—gritty red and orange sandstone, marble-white limestone, and crumbling blue-green shale—all lie atop one another in a breathtaking stack.

Visitors stand in awe as they take in the canyon's beauty and scale. You've seen pictures of the Grand Canyon before. It's hard to take a bad one! This is a place of almost unimaginable beauty. Sun and clouds dance over solid rock that seems never changing, but somehow always looks like it is. But no picture can ever replace the *feeling* you get standing by its vast majesty. To be there makes everything seem small—your body, your worries and fears, even your future or past. The quiet, peaceful hugeness of the canyon reminds us of how big Earth is. It also reminds us how Earth was here long before us, and how it will be here long after we are gone.

And yet, our place at the Grand Canyon is still important. How remarkable is it that today, this beautiful place belongs to the United States and its people. President Theodore Roosevelt declared the Grand Canyon to be the "one great sight that every

This famous portrait of President Theodore Roosevelt was painted by John Singer Sargent in 1903.

The Grand Canyon Visitor Center on the South Rim is just a short walk from the Rim Trail and one of the park's most famous viewing spots, Mather Point.

American should see."[3] U.S. citizens and international travelers alike still take the former president's advice. In 2015, over 5.5 million people visited Grand Canyon National Park.

Visitors can come to learn about the Grand Canyon's geology, history, plants and animals, and ancient cultures. They can take in the magnificent view. When they do, they, too, may be forever changed by this special place.

A DESERT VIEW

Most visitors enter Grand Canyon National Park by way of Tusayan. This village is just south of the canyon. The more scenic Desert View Drive enters the park from the east. Both routes bring tourists to the first big stop in the park: Desert View Visitor Center. The center includes an information building and the Watchtower, Trading Post, and Marketplace. The Watchtower features Native American culture. There, visitors can experience art, stories, and shows that celebrate area tribes.

Architect Mary Colter designed the Watchtower in 1932. Her design was inspired by the pueblos of the Anasazi people.

Chapter Two
A Grand
HISTORY

The first settlers in the Grand Canyon region were Native American tribes. Their descendants—the Navajo, Hopi, Havasupai, Hualapai, Zuni, and Yavapai—still call the Canyon home. Stone homes of these first settlers, some built more than 4,000 years ago, can still be seen today. They are tucked in caves in the canyon walls or perched on the canyon's rim. These peoples were also amazed by the canyon. They were certain it was crafted by gods. Its beauty inspired myths, such as this one from the Paiute tribe:

A long-ago chief loved his wife very dearly. His heart broke when she died; nothing seemed to ease his overwhelming grief. Seeing the chief in such despair, the god Taavotz decided to visit him. Taavotz promised that the chief's wife had moved on to a better place. If the chief promised to end his mourning, Taavotz would even take him to see her.

Native Americans carved out rooms from the rock high above the Colorado to store their food. Park archaeologists have found thousands of artifacts and sites so far, and they have only searched a small portion of the park.

The Paiute Indians tell a story of a fireball sent by a god to part the rocks of the Grand Canyon.

Taavotz rolled a giant ball of fire that parted the earth, crushing the mountains and crumbling the rocks. And so the Grand Canyon was made—a path straight through the earth to the spirit land. Taavotz walked down the path with the sad chief. Together they saw his wife, happy in the spirit land. The chief's heavy heart felt light once more, and he returned to his people.

But Taavotz worried that, if the chief spread word of the happiness that waited in the spirit world, his people would waste their lives trying to get there. So, Taavotz poured raging waters into the gorge, which we now call the Colorado River. Taavotz warned the chief that the powerful waters would drown anyone who tried to travel them.

In the harsh desert, the Grand Canyon must have seemed like a gift from the gods. Its steep-walled cliffs protected settlers from the angry sun for most of the day. The banks of the Colorado River held rich soil. There, people could plant beans, squash, melons, and corn. They hunted buffalo that roamed the high plains along the rim, using stone tools and carved arrowheads. They fished for the tasty chub that swam through the Colorado.

A roundtail chub.

García López de Cárdenas led an exploring party of Spanish soldiers to the Grand Canyon in 1540. They were the first Europeans to lay eyes on this natural wonder.

Tau-Gu (left), chief of the Paiutes, talks with John Wesley Powell in 1873.

These 19th-century prospectors hoped to find gold near Glen Canyon.

Native tribes may have warred with each other before recorded history, but they faced new battles when Spanish explorers arrived in the 1500s. The explorers sought gold and found precious little. Only priests settled in the Southwest. They tried to turn the native peoples away from their religions and toward Christianity. The tribes took these missionaries in, teaching them to herd sheep and weave blankets and clothes.

Arizona was part of Mexico in the 1820s, when American trappers came to hunt beavers for their valuable furs. The region had become a U.S. territory by the time explorer John Wesley Powell arrived in 1869. He called the magnificent gorge "the grand canyon."[1] By the 1880s, word had spread that valuable metals, especially copper and silver, lay beneath the Arizona desert. Prospectors—settlers who mined the land—traveled west hoping to strike it rich. Many failed, but soon realized the real treasure of the Southwest—its sunshine and natural beauty.

Railroads made their way to Arizona in 1887, bringing visitors from the eastern United States. Prospectors Ralph Henry Cameron and Pete and Martha Berry changed their minds about mining. Instead, they built hotels for tourists on Grand Canyon's South Rim.[2] Berry charged visitors one dollar to hike the beautiful Grandview Toll Road, a switchback trail down the canyon's walls. Likewise, Cameron guided hikers down the majestic Bright Angel Toll Road. Cameron also owned Indian Spring, the area's only source of clean water. Hikers had little choice but to cough up whatever coins Cameron asked for a much-needed drink.

The Santa Fe Railroad noticed the businessmen's success. They added a luxury hotel, the El Tovar. Between 1909–1910, the railroad built a grand depot at Grand Canyon Village.

So many visitors arrived that businesses had trouble keeping up. The U.S. government soon stepped in to protect the land and its visitors. President Benjamin Harrison declared the canyon a Grand Canyon Forest Reserve in 1893. In 1906, President Theodore Roosevelt declared it a game preserve. Despite these protections, settlers continued to mine the land, to

Traveling by train made it more affordable to visit the Grand Canyon. These first passengers rode from Williams, Arizona, to the Grand Canyon in 1901.

President Theodore Roosevelt visited the Grand Canyon in 1903. An active hunter and lover of the outdoors, Roosevelt was determined to preserve important lands for future generations.

hunt, and to chop down trees. Some predators, including mountain lions and wolves, were nearly wiped out.[3]

President Theodore Roosevelt forced all prospectors out when he declared the Grand Canyon a national monument in 1908. Finally, on February 26, 1919, Woodrow Wilson signed the bill that made the Grand Canyon the 15th National Park. The canyon's beauty and wildlife would be protected for generations to come.

JOHN WESLEY POWELL

John Wesley Powell (1834-1902) was a geology professor and Civil War veteran. In the spring of 1869, he became the first American to officially explore the Colorado River and through the Grand Canyon. Powell set off from the Wind River Range in Wyoming with nine men, four boats, and scientific instruments. The team survived hard times by befriending native tribes throughout the region, and learning some of their languages. They drifted down the steep Colorado River into the eastern end of Grand Canyon on August 5. Rough rapids through the canyon soon destroyed a boat and much of their food. By August 28, three of his men thought their captain was crazy. They left Powell's crew, hoping to climb out of the canyon on foot and find help. They were never seen again. Two days later on August 30, Powell and the six remaining men (of the original ten) cheered to see the canyon's end. Powell's expedition had successfully charted the course of the Colorado River, opening the Southwest to future settlers.[4]

Powell became the second director of the U.S. Geological Survey (1881–1894).

Chapter Three
Layers of Time:
Canyon Geology

It was not Taavotz's fiery ball that carved the Grand Canyon. Geologists believe the Canyon was carved, not by fire, but by water. Little by little, the Colorado River plucked away grains of earth as it traced the path of the canyon's floor.

The canyon starts at Lees Ferry (3,100 feet above sea level).[1] From there, the Colorado winds 277 miles through the canyon. The river runs from Lees Ferry to Lake Mead at an elevation of around 2,200 feet.

It rushes through sections of whitewater rapids that toss a boat like a toy. Meanwhile, other stretches of the river, even through the canyon, are smooth and gentle.

How long did it take the Colorado River to carve the Grand Canyon? When it was first discovered, explorers saw the Grand Canyon as proof of Noah's flood as described in the Bible. Scholars have many different theories when this event took place, but it could have happened between 2350–5000 BCE. That meant the canyon had to be less than 4,000 years old. As the canyon became

Lees Ferry, a historic site in northern Arizona, sits deep in canyon country. It is the only place for hundreds of miles where the canyon walls are low enough to allow travelers to cross the Colorado River.

more popular, geologists came from all over the world to study it. They understood that even the steep Colorado River needed millions of years to carry away a vertical mile of rock one piece at a time.

Geologists also thought about the movement of Earth's plates. Called tectonic plates, these pieces of broken crust make up Earth's surface. Arizona is on the North American Plate. Geologists believe that seventy million years ago, the entire Southwest was pushed skyward as the Pacific Plate shoved itself under the North American Plate. This motion formed the Rocky Mountains, as well as the high plains of the Southwest.

The Colorado River begins high in the Rocky Mountains at La Poudre Pass Lake, 10,184 feet high. It travels 1,450 miles through seven U.S. states and part of Mexico. Finally, it empties into the Gulf of California. The river follows a path through soft, weak rock. Over time, it sliced through layers of sandstone and limestone. It exposed the layers

The Rocky Mountains rise high over the American West, but none are taller than Mount Elbert in Colorado. It stands at 14,440 feet.

The Colorado River begins as a small lake at La Poudre Pass Lake. The trickle that starts here is on the Continental Divide. Some of its waters will flow west to become the Colorado River; the rest flow east to join the Mississippi River.

of colorful rock that now make up the Grand Canyon's walls, plateaus, and floor. Most geologists agree that the Colorado River began its path through the Grand Canyon area as little as five or six million years ago. However, some now think it may be fifteen, twenty-five, fifty, or even seventy million years old.[2,3] No matter when the Colorado River began its grand carving, the Grand Canyon is young compared to its ancient walls.

Like a birthday cake and a time capsule all in one, each of these rock layers represents a slice of time. Along some of the lowest parts of the canyon floor, the Vishnu Schist is revealed. This dark, folded, twisted layer dates back almost two *billion* years. As your eyes travel up the stripes ringing the canyon walls, it is like reading through time. The very youngest rocks lie at the rim. The Kaibab Limestone there formed 260 million years ago. At that time, Arizona lay mostly under a warm, shallow sea (like the Caribbean). There, embedded in the pale rock, fossils of shark teeth, shells, and worms have been found.

Just below the Kaibab's pale stripe lies the red-and-yellow Toroweap Sandstone. This layer formed 273 million years ago. The Toroweap represents ancient beaches, formed as the water level from the warm shallow sea rose and fell. The huge, cream-colored Coconino Sandstone below, formed 250 million years ago, is actually a layer of sand dunes

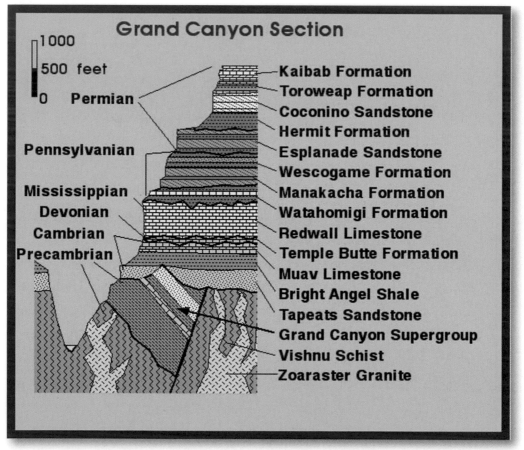

Grand Canyon Section

1000
500 feet
0   Permian
Pennsylvanian
Mississippian
Devonian
Cambrian
Precambrian

- Kaibab Formation
- Toroweap Formation
- Coconino Sandstone
- Hermit Formation
- Esplanade Sandstone
- Wescogame Formation
- Manakacha Formation
- Watahomigi Formation
- Redwall Limestone
- Temple Butte Formation
- Muav Limestone
- Bright Angel Shale
- Tapeats Sandstone
- Grand Canyon Supergroup
- Vishnu Schist
- Zoaraster Granite

Rock layers reveal slices of time through millions of years.

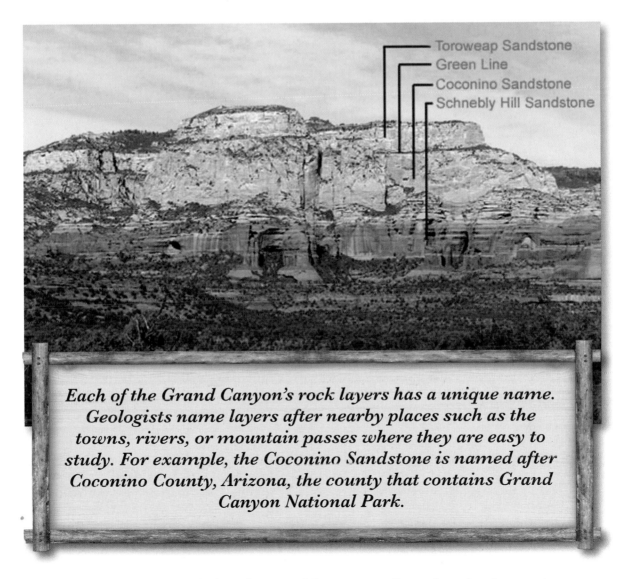

Toroweap Sandstone
Green Line
Coconino Sandstone
Schnebly Hill Sandstone

Each of the Grand Canyon's rock layers has a unique name. Geologists name layers after nearby places such as the towns, rivers, or mountain passes where they are easy to study. For example, the Coconino Sandstone is named after Coconino County, Arizona, the county that contains Grand Canyon National Park.

that have turned to solid rock. Fossil footprints found in this layer show that lizard-like animals once walked there, as did ancient scorpions and millipedes.

Taken together, these colorful stripes read like a book of Earth's history. They show that, over the past two billion years, what is now the Grand Canyon was once a beach, a river, and a sea. The land was even folded like dough as mountains rose nearby. When you stand at the canyon's edge, you might feel your lifetime is smaller than a grain of sand. But that is part of what makes the Grand Canyon one of the world's wonders. It is very rare to be able to see so much of Earth's geology exposed all at once. Wind and water may eventually erode all of the canyon rocks away. How special it is that we can be here, at this moment in time, to see these two billion years for ourselves.

Some of the Grand Canyon's rock layers were harder for the Colorado River to erode than others. These differences made beautiful features, such as Isis Temple (seen here), which reminded explorers of buildings in ancient Egypt.

THE TRAIL OF TIME

Two *billion* years? Geologic time can be difficult to understand. The Trail of Time can help. It offers a hands-on geology lesson right along the South Rim. This walking trail measures time as distance. It starts at the Yavapai Geology Museum with Year 0—today—and counts backward. A penny is embedded in the trail at every meter, representing *one million* years. Every ten meters, a bronze marker lies embedded instead. These are printed with dates marking *ten million* years. Samples of rock, collected from deep in the Canyon, are placed along the trail at their "birthdays."

Visitors can see and touch these samples. They show fossils of anemones and shells and even billion-year-old mudcracks.[4] After 2.83 miles of walking along the Trail of Time, you will have traveled back in time two billion years. That's when the oldest rocks, the Vishnu Schist, were deposited. Luckily, you also arrive at Grand Canyon Village, just in time for a well-deserved ice cream treat!

The Trail of Time is paved and fairly flat. It is handicap-accessible, and offers spectacular views of the Canyon. It can be a fun option for the whole family.

Folded Vishnu basement rock

A sample of Vishnu Schist for visitors to touch.

CHAPTER FOUR
WILD IN THE
CANYON?

Grand Canyon National Park seeks to preserve the land and its wildlife. Its mission is more important now than ever.

Dams are used to control the Colorado River, a precious source of water in the Southwest. The dams have changed the river and the animals that depend on it.

Wildlife in the Grand Canyon suffered almost as soon as the Glen Canyon Dam was built just upstream of Lees Ferry in 1964. The waters of the Colorado River once carried reddish sand to the canyon. The sand made muddy spots where fish and amphibians could lay their eggs. Now the Colorado's waters run clear. Without muddied waters, the river's bright silver fish are easy targets for predators. Fishermen have introduced such predator fish, like rainbow trout and striped bass, into the Colorado.

The dams have also changed the temperature of the river. The baking desert sun used to warm the water. In places, it would reach 80°F during the summer. Now, the

The enormous Glen Canyon Dam holds back the Colorado River, creating Lake Powell behind it.

Water behind the Glen Canyon Dam is released every so often as a "planned" flood, such as when lake levels rise too high, or, in 2008, to help save endangered river species.

river runs cold year-round, at a chilly 52°F. In this constant chill, fish eggs do not hatch as well, and food species don't thrive. Since the dam's construction, native species, like the humpback chub, have become endangered. Other fish species, including the squawfish and roundtail chub, have gone extinct.[1]

In March 2008, the U.S. government did something unusual to help save the fish: they staged a flood. Over the course of three days, water poured from doors in Glen Canyon Dam, cascading down the Grand Canyon at a rate of 2,600 gallons per minute. This was actually the third time since 1996 that the dam had been opened this way. The idea was to mimic the flooding that naturally occurs in the Colorado in times of heavy rain. These efforts seem to be working. Biologists report that the humpback chubs have increased their numbers by half since 2001. By 2009, around 7,650 chub were swimming in the waters of the canyon.[2]

Scientists use radio tags on mountain lions to track them through the canyon.

From hot, dry desert to chilly mountain forests, Grand Canyon National Park is home to many different habitats, each with many different species. Bobcats, coyotes, and mountain lions hunt in the brush. Lizards, from the striped eastern rail lizard to the spotted western whiptail, are small, quick, and fun to find. These reptiles stay very still and hidden to avoid becoming a tasty snack. They watch for raptors, snakes, and mammals like coyotes and foxes.

A lucky visitor might see one of the canyon's many snake species catching

Yellow-backed spiny lizards can grow up to twelve inches long. They come out of hiding to bask in the sun.

The Grand Canyon pink rattlesnake is not found anywhere else on Earth.

some sun atop a rock. Venomous reptiles are rare, like the black-and-orange Gila monster or Grand Canyon pink rattlesnake. However, Grand Canyon medics see few snakebites. Rattlesnakes would rather stay in the quiet desert brush and rocks than cross the busy hiking trails.

The most dangerous animal in the Grand Canyon is the rock squirrel. These lively critters have gray, brown, and white fur. They look like the squirrels many Americans see scampering across backyards. In the wild, rock squirrels eat fruit and seeds and tend to keep to themselves. But in the park, rock squirrels have squirmed their way into the spotlight.

It is illegal for park visitors to feed the animals, but at the South Rim, a typical summer's lunch for a rock squirrel might be a hand-fed feast of french fries. These smart beasts will shred cloth backpacks or picnic bags to get at people-food. Many squirrels at the most popular tourist sites have lost their fear of people, and they don't mind putting up a fight to get their food. Dozens of park visitors each year seek medical help for squirrel

Rock squirrels love to dart in for a meal, then retreat to a lookout spot to eat it.

bites. These can be especially dangerous, since the squirrels are known to carry rabies, hantavirus, and (in very rare cases) the bubonic plague.[3]

Grand Canyon visitors enjoy watching other curious mammals from a distance. Uinta chipmunks and cliff chipmunks scamper along the rim's edge. Mule deer and elk, especially females and their young, often munch on shrubs near the Verkamp Visitor Center. A mule deer can stand 3–3½ feet tall at the shoulder and weigh up to 300 pounds. Elk are larger, with males reaching 700 pounds. These sport shaggy hair under their necks.[4] Park law reminds visitors to keep a safe distance of at least 100 feet from all wild animals. Even the gentlest elk or deer can turn into charging freight trains during mating season (from August to early winter) or when calves are born in the spring.

On any sunny day, birds soar over the canyon. Smaller birds—such as the white-throated swift, the rock-colored canyon wren, and the bright mountain bluebird—tuck their nests into the junipers and pines of the rim forests. Some nest in rocky holes of the canyon itself.

Elk, such as this male (or bull), live in the pine forests of the canyon rim.

Vultures are easy to spot. Warm gusts of wind carried upward by the hot canyon bottom help to lift their wide black wings.[5]

The largest flying bird in North America also lives here—the California condor. "They are big vultures," says wildlife biologist Tami Courtney. "They're the ugliest bird when they're sitting still on a rock, but as soon as they take off and soar, they're the most amazing animals you're ever going to want to see—9½-foot wingspans soaring within five feet of your head, and you can hear the wind rustling through their feathers."[6]

The California condor's bare head actually helps it stay healthy, since the birds' dinner can't stick to its face.

Today the California condor is fighting for its life. In 1987, the U.S. Fish and Wildlife Service captured the only remaining twenty-two birds. They fed and cared for them, and bred the birds to protect their babies. Conservationists began releasing the birds back into the wild in 1992. By 2007, their numbers had grown to 279.[7] Today the 561 living California condors—116 in Grand Canyon National Park—represent a great success story.[8] With luck and patience, they will soar over the canyon for many years to come.

THE RAVEN

Native American myths tell of the legendary smarts of the raven, a common sight at the Grand Canyon. Today, flocks of ravens patrol Mather Campground. They waddle and caw to one another, working together to steal picnic leftovers.

The low, raspy caw! of the raven can be heard throughout the park. Their smarts are only matched by their skill in the air—ravens can fly upside down!

Chapter Five
Rim-to-Rim
ADVENTURE

Grand Canyon National Park has three distinct regions—the North Rim, the South Rim, and the difficult-to-reach Canyon Floor—but they might as well be other worlds. Though only an average of ten miles separates the North Rim from the South Rim, the gaping hole between them makes travel difficult. No bridges span the canyon within the park. It can take more than four and a half hours to drive the 212 miles from the visitor center of one rim to the other.

The South Rim stands at 7,000 feet in elevation, while the North Rim rises higher, to about 8,000 feet. This elevation difference makes the North Rim's climate wetter and colder. Winter snow and ice shut down this site between December and May.[1] The secluded North Rim sees few visitors. But in June and July, when the South Rim seems more crowded than Disney World, the North Rim calls to those who seek peace, quiet, and milder weather.

Looking for dry desert heat and blistering sunshine? Look no farther than the Canyon Floor. One mile separates

Wintertime along Bright Angel Trail sees few visitors, but beckons hikers who are prepared for snow and ice.

it from the top of the South Rim, but that mile straight down is enough to change the air from cool mountain forest to stony oven. On the floor, the average high in July is 106°F. In January at night, the thermometer can plummet to below freezing.[2]

Silver Bridge (front) and Black Bridge are the only Colorado River crossings on the canyon floor.

Baking in the sun at the canyon's bottom lies Phantom Ranch, a rustic lodge built in 1922 from wood and stone. The rooms are small and few, but guests enjoy air conditioning, heat, and running water—important luxuries in this harsh environment.

Getting to Phantom Ranch is half the fun. Only footpaths lead in or out. Many hikers enjoy walking down the 6.5-mile South Kaibab Trail. Others prefer the gentler 9.5-mile Bright Angel Trail.[3] Both trails descend from the South Rim into the canyon by a system of switchbacks. These zigzag paths are worn right into the canyon walls. Both trails offer views that can't be seen from the rim. Visitors can see and touch the canyon's walls as they go. But the trails are also unforgiving to rookie hikers.

On either trail, the hike from the South Rim to Phantom Ranch takes four to five hours. At first, it seems easy to walk downhill, but then the hot sun won't leave you alone. It beats down from all directions as it bounces off the canyon walls. Your muscles start to cramp from the constant motion— and that's before you realize that, eventually, you'll need to head back *up*.

The cozy Phantom Ranch has waited for tired hikers at the bottom of the Grand Canyon since 1922.

Most people don't realize that the change in elevation between the rim and floor will affect them, and in surprising ways. Many visitors aren't used to living at places that are 6,000 to 7,000 feet in elevation. At the Grand Canyon, high on the Colorado Plateau, the air actually has less oxygen. It drains the body of energy, making some people nauseous, tired, and hungry when they least expect it. The dry desert air saps water from the body, too. The canyon can fool even expert athletes, sometimes with deadly results.

On his visit in April 2009, Albert Shank, an experienced long-distance runner, wanted to complete a Rim-to-Rim run. He would run from the South Rim to the canyon bottom and then back up to reach the North Rim. He set out at a fast pace with a backpack full of water, energy bars, and peanut butter and jelly sandwiches. He made it down from the South Rim and just past Phantom Ranch when his legs began cramping. He nearly collapsed. Luckily, park rangers were around to rescue him and give him medical care.

"That was a rookie mistake, and I'm not a rookie," Shank said. "I learned that no matter how good of shape you're in, the canyon is something you need to respect, and dehydration will take you down."[4]

Instead of the grueling challenge of a Rim-to-Rim, or the weather extremes of the North Rim, most park visitors spend their entire trip at the South Rim. There, shoppers can browse one-of-a-kind stores and buy handmade Native American crafts right at the canyon's edge. Museum lovers can explore geology at the Yavapai Geology Museum, or view fine art at the Kolb Studio. Culture and history buffs can drive along Desert View to take in exhibits and live shows at the Watchtower. They can also explore the unearthed pueblo village at Tusayan.

Nearly everyone visits the Grand Canyon to get closer to nature. Many trails await. Whether taking the easy, flat Rim Trail or one of the many challenging and steep switchbacks, all you need is a pair of hiking boots, snacks, sunscreen, and all the water you can carry. Fill the day with canyon gazing, bird watching, and lizard spotting. Want to soar like a condor? For an unforgettable experience—while never leaving the ground—ride the Rim Trail on a bike. Speeding right next to the canyon makes you feel as if you're flying.

Yavapai Geology Museum gift shop.

At the end of a long day, vacationers can dine on buffalo steak and tuck into the soft sheets of the world-famous El Tovar Hotel. Campers can pitch their tents at Mather Campground and cook s'mores over a campfire while elk and mule deer wander calmly nearby. But just wait until the

El Tovar has received visitors since 1905.

stars come out. The South Rim is so high, dry, and far from cities, the night sky there gets dark enough to view the Milky Way with the naked eye. Whatever your adventure, the Grand Canyon offers a lifetime of wonder and fun for everyone.

Life and earth meet in peaceful beauty along the Rim Trail.

TRAINS, WHITEWATER RAFTS, AND...MULES?

Unusual Transportation at the Grand Canyon

TRAINS: Riding the Grand Canyon Railway today feels like a trip back in time to the Santa Fe Railroad in 1901. During the round-trip between Grand Canyon Village and Williams, Arizona, musicians travel from one car to the next. Don't be surprised if Wild West robbers "attack"! A marshal stands by, ready to save the day.

WHITEWATER RAFTING: Want to see the park from the river's view? Instead of navigating the swift, rushing waters with John Wesley Powell's heavy wooden boats, families today race along the rapids in large inflatable rafts. Watch out for the biggest rapid—Lava Falls. This section is short, but some call it "the scariest ten seconds on the river."[5] More than a dozen companies offer guided boat tours from the middle of April to early November.

MULE RIDES: Horses aren't the only heroes of the Wild West. Since the late 1800s, about one million people have traveled by mule in and out of the canyon. Today, mule riders must meet several requirements to be permitted to ride some of which include: they must must weigh less than 200–225 pounds (depending on the trail), stand over 57 inches tall, speak and understand fluent English, and not be afraid of heights or large animals.[6]

FUN FACTS

- Grand Canyon National Park was established on February 26, 1919, by President Woodrow Wilson.

- John Wesley Powell gave the park its name.

- The park is 277 miles long, eighteen miles wide, and one mile deep.

- It takes more than four and a half hours to drive the 212 miles from one rim to the other.

- The North Rim is 1,000 feet higher in elevation than the South Rim.

- The Colorado River includes at least 80 named rapids in the Grand Canyon.

- It takes only 20–25 seconds to travel the rapids at Lava Falls.

- Grand Canyon National Park contains over ninety mammal species, more than 447 bird species, and forty-one reptile and amphibian species.

- Six species of rattlesnakes can be found in the park. The most common is the Grand Canyon pink rattlesnake—and it is actually pink.

- The California condor has a wingspan of nearly 10 feet and can soar to a height of 15,000 feet. Since 1987, its population has increased from just twenty-two birds to more than 535.

- It is illegal to feed the animals in Grand Canyon National Park.

- The park contains more than 1,737 plant species.

- The Grand Canyon Skywalk is not actually in the park, but rather on the Hualapai Reservation. It extends seventy feet from the canyon rim and provides a clear view of the 4,000-foot drop to the Colorado River below.

- The average high temperature at the canyon floor in July is 106°F.

- The average low on the canyon's North Rim in January is 16°F.

Chapter Notes

Chapter 1. Meet the Canyon

1. Smithsonian Institution Museum of Natural History Global Volcanism Program, "Uinkaret Field," http://volcano.si.edu/volcano.cfm?vn=329010.
2. National Park Service, Grand Canyon National Park, "Park Statistics," https://www.nps.gov/grca/learn/management/statistics.htm.
3. Michael Joseph Oswald, *Your Guide to the National Parks* (Whitelaw, Wisconsin: Stone Road Press, 2012), p. 416.

CHAPTER 2. A Grand History

1. Becky Oskin, "The Story of the Canyon's Name," *Our Amazing Planet*, March 27, 2013, http://www.livescience.com/31903-amazing-grand-canyon-facts.html
2. Michael Anderson, *Polishing the Jewel: An Administrative History of Grand Canyon National Park*, (Grand Canyon, AZ: Grand Canyon Association, 2000), p. 8.
3. United Nations Educational Scientific and Cultural Organization, Grand Canyon National Park, http://whc.unesco.org/en/list/75
4. United States Geological Survey, "John Wesley Powell: Explorer, Geologist, Geographer"

CHAPTER 3. Layers of Time: Canyon Geology

1. Jeremy Schmidt, *Grand Canyon: A Natural History Guide* (New York: Houghton Mifflin Co., 1993), p. 166.
2. John Noble Wilford, "Study Says Grand Canyon Older Than Thought," *New York Times*, March 6, 2008.
http://www.nytimes.com/2008/03/06/science/06cnd-canyon.html?_r=2&hp&oref=slogin&oref=slogin
3. John Noble Wilford, "60-Million-Year Debate on Grand Canyon's Age," *New York Times*, November 29, 2012.
4. Trail of Time at the Grand Canyon National Park, http://www.trailoftime.org/what_is_it.html

CHAPTER 4. Wild in the Canyon?

1. Jeremy Schmidt, *Grand Canyon: A Natural History Guide* (New York: Houghton Mifflin Co., 1993), p. 171.

2. Brandon Loomis, "Endangered Grand Canyon Fish Making Comeback," *Salt Lake Tribune,* April 27, 2009.

3. NPS, "Keep Wildlife Wild."

4. NPS, "Elk," https://www.nps.gov/grca/learn/nature/elk.htm.

5. Jeremy Schmidt, *Grand Canyon: A Natural History Guide* (New York: Houghton Mifflin Co., 1993), pp. 189–190.

6. Jack Miles, "Grand Canyon Site of Woman's Condor Exploits," *Tribune Business News,* November 6, 2012.

7. Defenders of Wildlife, "California Condor," http://www.defenders.org/california-condor/basic-facts

8. Jack Miles, "Grand Canyon Site of Woman's Condor Exploits," *Tribune Business News,* November 6, 2012.

CHAPTER 5. Rim-to-Rim Adventure

1. NPS, Grand Canyon National Park, "Park Statistics," https://www.nps.gov/grca/learn/management/statistics.htm

2. Grand Canyon Treks

3. NPS, Grand Canyon National Park, "Hiking Frequently Asked Questions," https://www.nps.gov/grca/planyourvisit/hiking-faq.htm

4. Felicia Fonseca, "Grand Canyon Dangerous for Unprepared." Associated Press, June 19, 2009, http://www.nbcnews.com/id/31429349/ns/travel-active_travel/t/grand-canyon-dangerous-unprepared/

5. Arizona State University, "Lava Falls"

6. NPS, Grand Canyon National Park, "Mule Trips," https://www.nps.gov/grca/planyourvisit/mule_trips.htm

Books

Flynn, Sarah Wassner. *National Parks Guide USA.* Washington, DC: National Geographic Kids, 2012.

O'Connor, Jim. *Where Is the Grand Canyon?* New York: Grosset & Dunlap, 2015.

Ranney, Wayne. *Carving Grand Canyon: Evidence, Theories, and Mystery.* Grand Canyon, Arizona: Grand Canyon Association, 2012.

Robson, Gary D. *Who Pooped in the Park? Grand Canyon National Park: Scat and Tracks for Kids.* Helena, MT: Farcountry Press, 2005.

San Souci, Robert. "Origin Myths of the Grand Canyon." *Faces,* July/August 2008, Volume 24, Issue 10.

Stephenson, Midji. *Whose Tail on the Trail at the Grand Canyon?* Grand Canyon, AZ: Grand Canyon Association: 2012.

On the Internet

Flight Through the Grand Canyon
    https://www.nps.gov/grca/learn/photosmultimedia/fly-through.htm
Geology for Kids: The Grand Canyon
Grand Canyon Discovery: NPS Views
Grand Canyon National Park Official Kids' Page
    https://www.nps.gov/grca/learn/kidsyouth/index.htm
Grand Canyon Railway and Hotel: The Train
    http://www.thetrain.com/the-train/

Works Consulted

Allen, Thomas B., et al. *Guide to National Parks of the United States.* Washington, DC: National Geographic, 2012.

Anderson, Michael. *Polishing the Jewel: An Administrative History of Grand Canyon National Park.* Grand Canyon, AZ: Grand Canyon Association, 2000.

Arizona State University. "Lava Falls."

Defenders of Wildlife—http://www.defenders.org/

Fodor's Travel Service. *Arizona & The Grand Canyon.* New York: Fodor's Travel, 2016.

Fonseca, Felicia. "Grand Canyon Dangerous for Unprepared." Associated Press, June 19, 2009, http://www.nbcnews.com/id/31429349/ns/travel-active_travel/t/grand-canyon-dangerous-unprepared/

Grand Canyon National Park

Grand Canyon Treks

Loomis, Brandon. "Endangered Grand Canyon Fish Making Comeback." *Salt Lake Tribune*, April 27, 2009.

Mathls, Allyson, and Carl Bowman. "The Grand Age of Rocks: The Numeric Ages for Rocks Exposed within Grand Canyon." National Parks Service, 2006

Miles, Jack. "Grand Canyon Site of Woman's Condor Exploits." *Tribune Business News*, November 6, 2012.

Oskin, Becky. "The Story of the Canyon's Name." *Our Amazing Planet,* March 27, 2013, http://www.livescience.com/31903-amazing-grand-canyon-facts.html

Oswald, Michael Joseph. *Your Guide to the National Parks.* Whitelaw, Wisconsin: Stone Road Press, 2012.

Polak, Monique. "The Lure of the Grand Canyon; Hikers Who Descend Below the Rim Discover One of the Most Beautiful Places on Earth." *The Gazette* (Montreal, Quebec), March 10, 2012.

Schmidt, Jeremy. *Grand Canyon: A Natural History Guide.* New York: Houghton Mifflin, 1993.

Smithsonian Institution Museum of Natural History Global Volcanism Program. "Uinkaret Field," http://volcano.si.edu/volcano.cfm?vn=329010.

Trail of Time at the Grand Canyon National Park.

United Nations Educational Scientific and Cultural Organization. "Grand Canyon National Park." http://whc.unesco.org/en/list/75.

United States Geological Survey. "John Wesley Powell: Explorer, Geologist, Geographer."

Wilford, John Noble. "Study Says Grand Canyon Older Than Thought." *New York Times*, March 6, 2008.

Wilford, John Noble. "60-Million-Year Debate on Grand Canyon's Age." *New York Times*, November 29, 2012. http://www.nytimes.com/2012/11/30/science/earth/study-sees-older-grand-canyon-stirring-controversy.html?_r=0

conservationist (kon-ser-VAY-shuh-nist)—A person who promotes the protection of and of natural resources.

dehydration (dee-hy-DRAY-shun)—A dangerous loss of water from the body.

erode (ee-ROHD)—Gradually worn away by water, wind, or other natural means.

geological (jee-uh-LAH-jih-kul)—Dealing with rocks and soils.

gorge (GORJ)—A narrow canyon with steep, rocky walls, especially one through which water runs.

hydroelectric (hy-droh-ee-LEK-trik)—A system that generates electricity using the energy from falling water.

limestone (LYM-stohn)—White or gray stone formed when mud is deposited in still waters.

missionary (MIH-shun-air-ee)—A person who tries to spread a certain religion, usually to people in other countries or cultures.

prospector (PROS-pek-tor)—Someone who hunts for minerals.

rapid (RAP-id)—A part of a river where the current runs swiftly and is very rough.

reserve (ree-ZERV)—Protected land.

rustic (RUS-tik)—Built in a simple way using nearby materials.

sandstone (SAND-STOHN)—Rock formed from sand.

schist (SHIST)—Rock with coarse crystals formed from high heat and pressure deep within the earth.

shale (SHAYL)—Dark gray, blue, or green rock formed from mud or silt deposited in still waters.

switchback (SWITCH-bak)—A path or road that turns sharply back and forth to make a steep climb slower and gentler.

tectonic plates (tek-TAH-nik PLAYTS)—Continent-sized pieces of Earth's crust.

venomous (VEH-nuh-mus)—Poisonous.

PHOTO CREDITS: P.1—Marcin Wichary; pp. 4, 15, 18, 29, 31, 37—NPS.gov; p. 6—Realbrvhr; pp. 8, 9, 34—Michael Quinn, NPS.gov; p. 10—Drenaline; p. 13—Ferrer Dalmau; p. 20—Rick Kimpel; p. 24—Lucca Galluzzi; p. 26—Dave Fulmer; p. 28—Usa.gov; p. 30—Chris Amelung; p. 32—US Fish and Wildlife Services; p. 33—Aaron; pp. 38, 39— Grand Canyon National Park; p. 47—Moyan Brenn. All other photos—Public Domain. Every measure has been taken to find all copyright holders of material used in this book. In the event any mistakes or omissions have happened within, attempts to correct them will be made in future editions of the book.

Index